Talk About the Elephant

WRITTEN BY

DANIEL BLAKESLEE

ILLUSTRATED BY

DARLINE HOLMES

DEDICATION

For our mothers, who are now with Jesus,
Helen Blakeslee and Ellia Holmes.

ACKNOWLEDGMENTS

This book is designed for Financial Peace University® dropouts or those FPU graduates who need a little direction. If your Debt Snowball is Melting, your Emergency Fund needs to go to the ER, or if you tripped while trying to take some baby steps, then maybe this book can help.

For my countless students and counseling clients who had to endure my dry sense of humor. May your debt snowball not roll you over, and may your 401k never again be a 201k. Keep making a difference.

In this world of coins and
bills so bright,
Let's talk about saving,
it will be such a delight.

Put pennies in piggy banks,
save, save, save,
Add those shiny quarters,
make your money behave.

For a rainy day,
it's a wise old notion,
To stash some cash in
your savings portion.

Dimes and nickels,
they all have a role,
In building your savings,
to reach your goal.

With dollars in jars and
cash in a stack,
You'll soon see your
savings begin to attract.

Interest will make it grow like
a flower in May,
And you'll be prepared
for that rainy day.

So skip the stop at the corner store,
for that fancy latte,
Save a little more,
put some cash away,

When storm clouds
gather and skies turn gray,
You'll have your umbrella,
and cash, come what may.

So remember, my friend,
as you go on your way,
To save for tomorrow,
and for a brighter today.

For when life brings you rain
and skies turn to gray,
Your savings will shine,
and troubles melt away.

In the land of green dollars,
so crisp and so grand,
Let's talk about saving,
it's just as we planned.

For emergencies lurking,
around the next bend,
Save a week's pay,
to be your loyal, dear friend.

So start with some cash,
a one some zeros,
In your savings stash,
where your treasure grows.

With discipline and patience,
and a plan to obey,
You'll reach your grand goal,
come what may.

Skip the splurges,
and the impulse to spend,
A week's pay saved for peace,
definitely a wise money trend.

When life throws a curveball,
you'll be okay,
With a rainy day fund
to brighten your day.

No need for worry,
no need for despair,
Your savings can protect you,
like a big momma bear.

A week's pay saved,
a safety bouquet,
For life's unexpected,
come what may.

So remember this rule,
as you go on your way,
Save for those dark moments,
for a brighter today.

With money stashed away,
a rainy day fund, hip, hip hooray,
You'll survive the unexpected,
come what may.

In a room filled with chatter,
laughter, and glee,
There's an elephant lurking,
maybe you can't see.

It's big and it's heavy,
yet no one dares say,
"Let's discuss this big issue,
right here, today!"

Its name is debt,
about which we don't want to talk.
We're going to keep quiet,
it doesn't exist if about we talk not.

It stands in the corner,
with a trunk that's so long,
But we pretend it's not there,
oh, what's going on?

We dance 'round the subject,
we tiptoe with care,
Ignoring the elephant,
with talk of debt in the air.

Its presence is felt in every hush,
a whisper of debt in each puff,
Yet we act like it's not there,
it's really quite tough.

Let's break down the walls,
let's make some space,
To talk about the elephant,
face to face.

For the elephant carries
a debt crisis within,
A truth that we're hiding,
it's time to begin.

To acknowledge our debt,
to find a new way,
To deal with the issue,
come what may.

So let's gather our courage,
be brave, and be bold,
Let's address our debt problem,
let the truth be told.

In the room full of whispers,
let honesty bloom,
For facing the issue,
dispels all the gloom.

In the room of our homes,
there's something quite clear,
The elephant lurking,
let's bring it all here.

It's debt, my dear friend,
the elephant so grand,
With loans and bills piling up,
it's time to understand.

It starts with a credit card,
so shiny and bright,
But the interest keeps growing,
oh, what a fright.

It grows and it lingers,
like an elephant's size,
But ignoring the problem
won't be very wise.

We buy this, we charge that,
oh, the spending spree,
Till we're buried in debt,
can't you see what I see?

It's time to address it,
no more room to presume,
Debt's the elephant in the room,
let the talking resume!

In a world of wild spending,
let me relate,
A tale of extravagance,
oh, it's not too late.

Spending on televisions,
shoes, and clothes so fine,
We spent like crazy,
oh, isn't that a sign.

We bought the biggest
TV screen in town,
With pixels so sharp,
so we could see the touchdown.

And motorcycles with
engines that roar,
Zooming through life,
like never before.

New shoes and new clothes,
a new outfit each day,
For every occasion,
for all to say, "Hooray!"

Designer labels,
oh, we couldn't resist,
Our closets so full,
we couldn't see the twist.

But soon, the bills piled up
like a tower so high,
But then, debt knocked on the door,
oh, my, oh, my!

The wild spending spree
had a price to pay,
As debts grew and grew,
Oh, they rue the day.

So heed this tale,
my friends, take a pause,
Before spending wildly,
you should know the cause.

Budget and save,
be mindful and wise,
So you won't fall into
that debt-filled disguise.

Televisions and motorcycles,
shoes, and attire,
Can be enjoyed,
but not when they make life dire.

Keep your spending in check,
that's the key,
To a life that's more happy,
by living debt-free!

With a budget in hand and
some discipline, too,
We can tame this big elephant,
it's what we must do.

Cut down on expenses,
save more than we spend,
And bit by bit, that elephant,
we'll mend.

So let's face our finances
with courage and joy,
And tackle that debt,
and teach each girl and boy.

For when we're debt-free,
we'll feel light and not doom,
No more elephant in the room,
only the joy of a financial boom.

Once the rainy day fund
is in its secure place,
It's time to tackle debt,
with a smile on your face.

Two methods to choose from,
let's explore them anew,
The Debt Snowball or Avalanche,
it's all up to you.

The Snowball's quite friendly,
it starts oh so small,
You pay off small debts first,
then increase to the tall.

With each debt you conquer,
a victory's won,
Building confidence,
paying them off one by one.

Then comes the Debt Avalanche,
fierce and so bold,
You tackle high-interest debts,
and the story unfolds.

You'll save more on interest,
it's a strategic feat,
Paying down debts faster,
isn't that neat?

With each payment you make,
you'll feel more in control,
As your debt amount shrinks,
you'll accomplish your goal.

The Snowball or Avalanche,
the choice is your own,
To clear up your debts,
till they're fully undone!

No matter the method,
keep focused and true,
With discipline and patience,
you'll see it all through.

Once debt's in the past,
you'll feel oh so light,
Your future's much brighter,
oh, what a sight.

So take up the challenge,
it's time to ignite,
The debt-free journey,
it's a beautiful flight.

With Snowball or Avalanche,
you'll soon be debt-free,
A happier future,
for your family and thee.

Once debt's in the rearview,
you'll see, it's so neat,
The path to new goals,
you'll be able to compete.

Now, the kid's college awaits,
with knowledge so vast,
Let's save for the future,
That'll sure be a blast!

Put pennies in jars,
stack your dollars with care,
For higher education,
it's a journey to bear.

With each nickel and dime,
and each coin in your tote,
You'll build your savings,
for college without a note.

And after you've paid for
that college degree,
Why not treat yourself,
Now that you're able to see!

Retirement?
Or a boat on the water,
where you'll sail wild and be free.

With discipline and savings,
it's quite the adventure,
For major purchases,
with purpose and venture.

So save up your cash,
watch it grow day by day,
For college and boats,
in your own special way.

With a heart full of dreams and
a wallet that floats,
You'll reach your goals,
as you sail in debt free boats!

USS L.E. Phant

The lessons of savings,
they're timeless and true,
Tame the elephant and make it a pet
Debt isn't needed
to buy something new.

With patience and planning,
and savings goals to denote,
You'll reach for the stars,
in your very own boat.

In a house with a mortgage,
so grand and so tall,
There's a tale to be told,
let's share it with all.

With patience and planning,
let's embark on a quest,
To pay off that mortgage,
So we can live at our best.

You won't be house poor,
when you get the key to the door!

Make extra payments,
just a little each day,
Chip away at that debt,
don't let it delay.

With each extra dollar,
you'll come closer, you'll see,
To a debt-free house,
where you'll dance with such glee.

Refinance if you can,
for a lower interest rate,
And save on those payments,
Yep, it's going to be great.

Apply windfalls and bonuses,
don't let them slip,
Into the abyss of spending,
help your mortgage get a grip.

As the years pass you by,
the balance will shrink,
The interest reduced,
it's like magic, I think.

And one sunny day,
a debt-free house will be yours,
With open arms,
it'll welcome you through its doors.

No more monthly payments,
it's such a delight,
Your house is now truly your own,
day and night.

With the mortgage retired,
you'll surely be free,
To enjoy your sweet home,
debt-free as can be.

So remember, dear friend,
remember my rhyme,
To pay off your mortgage,
it just takes some time.

With discipline and focus,
and a plan so astute,
You'll achieve your dream home,
it's really quite cute!

Living without debt,
it's a feeling so sweet,
A life full of joy,
from your head to your feet.

No more bills to be paid,
no creditors in sight,
It's a marvelous feeling,
oh, what a delight.

You're free as a bird,
with a skip in your stride,
No more worries or stress,
No bill collectors to hide.

Your finances are tidy,
your budget's a breeze,
Living without debt,
you'll do as you please.

No more interest payments,
no more loans to repay,
Your money is yours,
it's here to stay.

You'll save and you'll invest,
for your future so bright,
With no debt to hold you,
you're ready to take flight.

You'll sleep like a baby,
all through the night,
No debt-induced nightmares,
you'll sleep so tight.

Your dreams are your own,
they'll come true, you'll see,
Living without debt,
you'll feel wild and free.

So embrace this feeling,
this wonderful sensation,
Of a life without debt,
it's a grand celebration.

With financial freedom,
you'll feel so complete,
Living debt-free,
it can't be beat.

Now in conclusion,
this is no illusion...

In the world of finance,
let's make a plan,
A financial adventure,
for every woman and man.

First, save one week's pay,
for the skies so gray,
To keep troubles at bay,
during a rainy day.

Next, create a budget,
with a zero base, it's so neat,
Live within your means,
it's really a treat.

Track every expense,
watch where your cash goes,
You'll find financial freedom,
with fewer worries and woes.

Now, let's tackle your debts,
like a snowball we roll,
Start with the smallest,
meet your financial goal.

With each debt you conquer,
like a victory dance,
You'll build confidence and
give debt no chance.

Emergency fund,
it's the next smart move,
For life's unexpected,
it'll help you improve.

Three to six months' expenses,
put that cash away,
You'll sleep sound at night,
come what may.

Invest for your future,
let your money take flight,
In stocks or in bonds,
it's a long-term delight.

With patience and time,
your wealth will accrue,
Your financial future,
it's all up to you.

So, remember this wonderful tale
of finance and fun,
To save, budget, and conquer debt,
it all can be done.

With an emergency fund and
savings so bright,
Your financial future
will be a beautiful sight!

THE END

ABOUT THE AUTHOR

Daniel Blakeslee is known for his bestselling book, "Lead on Purpose." He is a passionate and enthusiastic speaker, author, counselor, and coach. He believes coaching and training is his way to serve others. He was trained by Dave Ramsey* and his team as a financial coach; that together with his 3 decades of pastoral counseling experience allows him to bridge the gap from where you are to where you want to be.

He was a highly decorated leader in the United States military; having served on several submarines. Daniel developed the pilot course for the Navy's Total Quality Management and Leadership training program. He has excelled in non-profit leadership and has authored several books on leadership training and development. He serves as marriage counselor and mentor, and is currently writing several books on relationships.

*Completion of Dave Ramsey's Financial Coach Master Training does not create an employment or agency relationship with Ramsey Solutions or its affiliates, it does not constitute a license or credentials to engage in legal, tax, accounting, investment or other profession, nor does it constitute an endorsement or recommendation of the Coach by Dave Ramsey.

www.ingramcontent.com/pod-product-compliance
Lightning Source LLC
LaVergne TN
LVHW081336060426
835513LV00014B/1309